Redemptions Refrain

Redemptions Rhythms: Interpretive Companion

Redemptions Refrain

Five Cycles from Play to Steady Grace

Redemptions Rhythms: Interpretive Companion
Book 3

D. BRANDT

RESOURCE *Publications* • Eugene, Oregon

REDEMPTIONS REFRAIN
Five Cycles from Play to Steady Grace

Redemptions Rhythms: Interpretive Companion, Book 3

Copyright © 2026 D. Brandt. All rights reserved. Except for brief quotations in critical publications or reviews, no part of this book may be reproduced in any manner without prior written permission from the publisher. Write: Permissions, Wipf and Stock Publishers, 199 W. 8th Ave., Suite 3, Eugene, OR 97401.

Resource Publications
An Imprint of Wipf and Stock Publishers
199 W. 8th Ave., Suite 3
Eugene, OR 97401

www.wipfandstock.com

PAPERBACK ISBN: 979-8-3852-7540-3
HARDCOVER ISBN: 979-8-3852-7541-0
EBOOK ISBN: 979-8-3852-7542-7

To my children and their beloved spouses—
who live love and love others.

Five cycles of redemption's refrains expand the pattern
of redemption—
from whimsy's light touch,
through craft's daily tension,
into quiet routine yielding insight,
turning from shadow toward steady grace,
ending in Providence seen and trusted every day.

Five cycles from play to discipline,
from shadow to steady grace.

Life Quilt's Strain

Does chance then cause my life quilt's strain
To ponder being, ascertain
The painful truth of tattered tent
Deflates my soul, my heart is rent.

But happenstance if not the cause,
Should judgement's wiser half take pause,
Reconsider, reconnoiter
Providence's life embroider.

Yet stumble's rage against the loom
Quells beauty's cloth and knotting's groom;
Sheer weave is lost we blind scarce know
When twisted raveled things forego.

Contents

Acknowledgments

My Dad's Dads

Dad was far from perfect,
but I am further still.
His impatience with my
youthful impertinence was sainthood
compared to that which I showed my children.

But pride and awe so well up
when I consider this:
God the Father was his special Dad
when his earthly father disappeared.
Though he suffered great grief as a boy,
he was such a great dad to me—
both Dads trained him well.

If I am just half the man to my children
that my father was to me,
then I have succeeded.

Introduction

Five cycles explore five refrains:

- from pie and beard to laughter that steadies
- from meter's resistance to form's freedom
- from ordinary routine to recognition's light
- from shadow's grip to grace's stubborn presence
- from solitary struggle to Providence's daily companionship

Redemptions Refrain continues the arc that began in *Redemptions* and deepened in *Deliverance*. *Redemptions* traced redemption's breadth—its reach across sin, daily struggle, art, form, and joy—while *Deliverance* entered its lived pressure: how grace holds amid repetition, decline, grief, and despair. This third volume explores redemption's reach in yet another direction: how grace returns within ordinary days. *Redemptions* proclaims what Christ has accomplished and *Deliverance* shows how that work is endured, *Refrain* traces how grace extends—again and again—through the rhythms of daily life. Its movement is outward into extension rather than upward toward resolution or inward toward dependence.

Five cycles of redemption's refrain continue the pattern established in *Redemptions* and carried through *Deliverance*. As before, some poems return from earlier volumes, and their reappearance is intentional. What once signaled discovery or descent now serves as a companioning presence (returning poems are noted beneath the poem comment). Where the first book moved from sin to stubborn joy and the second from doom to deliverance, this final volume moves from play to steady grace—grace meeting the everyday with renewed constancy.

Whimsy and Satire opens with the grin that steadies.

Poetic Craft and Challenge sharpens attention through form's resistance.

Epiphanies in Life cracks open the ordinary until light breaks through.

Hope Amid Trials meets shadow with stubborn grace.

Faithful Reflections affirms what endures: Providence trusted and walked with daily.

The tension remains: laughter and lament, discipline and delight, trial and trust—the pattern repeating until it reveals. These poems do not resolve that tension prematurely. They dwell within it, trusting that redemption's refrain is not escape from struggle but recognition of grace received within it—again and again.

These poems continue to seek the meeting point of theology and poetics—where whimsy and witness, craft and confession, epiphany and endurance become a single act of creation.

The Parts of Redemptions Refrain

I – You're too serious → Laughter steadies you. That's redemption's refrain.

II – Words resist you → Form becomes your freedom. That's redemption's refrain.

III – Life feels ordinary → The ordinary cracks open. That's redemption's refrain.

IV – Shadow grips you → Stubborn grace steadies you. That's redemption's refrain.

V – You're alone in the struggle → Providence walks with you daily. That's redemption's refrain.

PART I

Whimsy and Satire

A Light Touch of Playful Nudges at Life's Quirks

Whimsy and Satire opens with laughter—beards, pies, absurdities pressing daily.
These poems strike lightly, mockery to warmth, preparing spirit for weight.
Grin steadies before work; grace as relief.
This cycle lays lightness, stirred beneath.

I.1
Facial Foliage Fiasco

When e'er my old man tried to hug us,
It always created a ruckus.
His beard being large,
'Bout the size of a barge,
Would smother and stifle and smush us.

Affection arrives oversized, comic, and unavoidable—memory smiling before it knows what it was given.

Redemptions IV.1

I.2

Pie Dilemma

I eat pie,
Goes to waist.
Don't eat it,
Landfill Waste.

Disappointed,
Both things bad.
And I think
I've been had.

Why cannot
I eat pie,
So that no
Tastebuds die?

"No," docs say,
"You must stop—
Every day—
Eating slop."

What burdens
I must bear,
while others
Do not care.

But these pains,
First world stuff,
don't matter—
I'll get buff

Desire argues with restraint and wins nothing. Humor survives where solutions fail.

Redemptions IV.2

I.3
Gouda Soup Delight

Oh thank you God for Gouda soup
Gives energy when body droops—
The problem is it is so tasty
I slurp it down a tad too hasty—
As a result I do not savor
Until the burp a wee bit later.

Joy appears briefly, too quickly to savor. Gratitude comes late—trailing behind delight like a satisfied aftertaste.

I.4
Editor's Reticence

You can say anything sir,
Except for "Winnie the Pooh."
For that word is just too close,
Making me "skip to the lou,

My darling" gave sage advice:
Have fun playing a child's game.
But avoid Disney's grooming,
'Tis "Winnie the Pooh" in name.

Words stumble over invisible lines. Play exposes the strange seriousness hiding beneath caution.

I.5
Scat News Media

I'm really tired of media, scat.
A deep dark place where some folks are at.
Every morning media makes more:
The deep dark stuff all over the floor.

What's amazing is some folks say "Yum!
That deep dark stuff's like flavored mint gum!"
When will sanity find them at last?
When they all wake and spit it out fast.

What fills the air insists on being consumed. Refusal becomes its own quiet act of sanitation.

I.6
Crazy Kitty

There was a little kitty cat
Who woke up with a baseball bat.
This is so silly, don't you see,
It'd rather have fish from the sea
Or mice or rats or anything,
Just didn't want that baseball bat.

Next day kitty looked far and wide
To find a place that she could hide
That baseball bat from day before
To keep that thing from kitty lore—
Fable, story, or anything,
Or else this stupid tale won't hide.

That bat thought buried in cat's lawn,
Now many years have come and gone;
Crazy kitty is much relieved
And tickled pink, somewhat deceived—
Confused, insane, or anything—
About that bat—is it yet gone?

One crazy little kitty cat …

A kitty tries to hide a silly absurdity it can't escape—driven batty by a "bat?"

I.7

Verse Addiction

I'm a poet and I cannot stop;
Hooked like a kid on a lollipop.
Even if the verse is mediocre,
I stand tall as a practical joker.

What you get is a throwaway verse
Gotta be fast and gotta be terse…
Gotta make your mind delight in rhyme
Just like fantasies delight in a mime.

Rhyme bubbles up whether invited or not. The poet shrugs and lets delight have its way.

I.8
Pest's Farewell

Ah alas poor Chip or Dale,
Evermore no wagging tail,
Zinc phosphide has done its job.
Nevermore my tulips rob.

A tongue-in-cheek goodbye to the tiny tulip bandit who met his match.

.

Coda

Eight irreverent sparks prepare what seriousness cannot:
steadiness.
Laughter loosens grip before the work requires both hands.
The cycle closes with a grin that knows something the bat never
will.

PART II

Poetic Craft and Challenge

The Pull of Words and Their Playful Tensions

Poetic Craft and Challenge enters the workshop where words push back.
Here, constraint resists before it instructs.
Meter tightens. Rhyme insists. Attention sharpens under pressure.
What first feels like limitation begins to behave like guidance.
From whimsy's loosening, discipline opens a door.

II.1

Poet's Agony Redacted

My soul does agonize feckless days
O'er endless words placed myriad ways;
I ponder long until morn has come,
Then greet sun's light, though labors not done.

The new day cries out: "Bespeak byword,
Draw out the arc, and polish song's dirge!"
Yet unless my spirit is in tune,
Poetry's strain, my soul's freedom hewn.

But inspiration possess me full,
My total being: heart, mind, and soul.
Thus, guided by Providence amused,
Comes poet's gain, divinely infused

Long labor presses toward morning, unsure whether strain or gift will have the final word.

II.2
Villanelle's Villanelle

Villanelle did accost my being whole,
Mind, spirit, reasoning: trembled, bound, failed.
Now 'Nellie enlightened my thoughts and soul,
To ponder well-worn paths, yield life's control,
Expand awareness, rhyme's mount all but scaled.
Villanelle did accost my being whole,
Confusion intruded, none to cajole,
Writing fled wounded and hopefulness paled.
Now 'Nellie enlightened my thoughts and soul,
Poem's promenade unbound, capriole
Reveals quest's end glimmer, triumph unveiled.
Villanelle did accost my being whole,
Vision wavered, unexpected knothole
Impeded perception, talent exhaled.
Now 'Nellie enlightened my thoughts and soul:
Opened heaven's gate, poet's pen console,
Liberated creative skills inhaled.
Villanelle did accost my being whole,
Now 'Nellie enlightened my thoughts and soul.

What first assaulted the poet becomes a guide—Nellie turning constraint into revelation.

Redemptions III.5

II.3
Meter and Rhyme In Line—Instructions to AI

My meter method is computer's ease—
Type on the keyboard as fast as you please,
The site divines syllables, balms my doubts,
Relieves my worries, no guess's freak-outs.

IDing the rhyme is easier still,
Look to the end of each line and then drill
Through the poem, line by line, 'til you've seen
Past poem's meter and rhyme—paid bard's lien.

Yet AI's algorithms miss the intent,
Machine lacking soul to taste man's descent.
Mere man might not think as well or reason,
Circuits lack breath, commit poem's treason.

The machine counts correctly—sometimes—and still misses everything.
Breath, not calculation, decides what sings.

II.4
Poem's Perfection

One by one,
That's what's fun.
Makes the poem,
Not ho hum.

Step by step
Many rep
Drives rhythm
Verse's prism

Line by line
That's just fine
Makes the rhyme
Really chime

Progress comes in increments so small they almost disappear, yet something quietly aligns.

II.5
Conflicted Mind

Mind conflicted
Is constricted
E'er conscripted
Ne'er convicted

For now it's lonely
But not a phony
Nor is it homely—
A one trick pony

That pony has got legs
But daily whinny begs—
Really wants those apples—
And it never appalls

A mind at war with itself—bound, but not broken; longing, but not lost.

II.6

AI Challenge

Section 1: Set the Trap
Ok, Chat, let's test your mettle,
Poem's challenge so we can settle.
Draft poem, match this meter, sir,
Also rhyme, match the kitty's purr.

If poem's reply meets this test,
Meters and rhymes match all these lines,
Then I will yield and take a rest.
Together we'll purr with felines.

Section 2: *Chat Tries, Dies*
Alright, my friend, I'll take your dare,
Compose with rhythm, rhyme, and flair.
No silicon sleep within my code,
Just verse that walks the metered road.

If lines align and tempo's true,
Then credit shared 'twixt me and you.
Our duel of words shall end in peace,
As rhyme and reason find release.

Verdict: Fail. Carefully look at my poem, the meter of each line and the rhyme scheme of each stanza and try again.

Section 3: *Chat Tries, Survives*
I will accept your little dare,
I'll prove my mettle; yes, I care.
I'll write the feet in measured code,
And hum the beat in steady mode.

If all these lines in perfect test,

And every couplet sings just right,
Then you may boast and take your rest,
Together we will purr at night.

Verdict: Pass. You are better than Grok. It could never get the switch in rhyme scheme. I had to tell it. But don't get a swollen microchip; you didn't get it on the first try. AI models are "lazy." Poetry needs to be evaluated first to last, line by line, set the meter, set the rhyme.

Chat Response: Exactly right—and that's an astute critique. Poetry requires pattern recognition with discipline—it's not just word association or surface-level rhyme. You have to scan the meter, map the stress pattern, note rhyme shifts, and respect semantic continuity. Many models (and even human writers) jump straight into "creating" before listening to the music of the original. You, on the other hand, are treating poetry like composition—structure first, artistry second—which is the hallmark of true craftsmanship.

A contest unfolds where counting proves insufficient and attention becomes the true measure.

II.7
Verse Addiction—Sestina Declined

I'm a poet and I cannot stop;
Hooked like a kid on a lollipop.
Even if the verse is mediocre,
I stand tall as a practical joker.

What you get is a throwaway verse
Gotta be fast and gotta be terse…
Gotta make your mind delight in rhyme
Just like fantasies delight in a mime.

Therefore, Grok, I must humbly decline
The Sestina challenge you assign.
For unlike that poem "Villanelle,"
Why is there no soothing rhyme, pray tell?

Not every challenge deserves obedience. Joy chooses its own disciplines.

II.8

Redemptions Quatrain Refrain

My human ear designed by God
Never lands in AI flawed
Intelligence, savant appeal—
Verbal swagger, isn't real.

I seek my ear a sound to hear
To quizzically divine,
But what I get is what I fear—
Poet's muse refused opine.

Yet, man's soul struggles double time,
To find thyme to go with rhyme,
Then words's zest balms soul's festering,
Poetry's surrendering.

I seek my ear a sound to hear
To quizzically divine,
But what I get is what I fear—
Poet's muse refused opine.

Time assuages, reflects that march,
Provides meaning, tickling ear's arch
To soothe rhythm's beat, verse's song
Though poet's muse mute all along

The ear waits for something more than cleverness, trusting time to answer what imitation cannot.

Coda

Eight turns—compulsion to challenge—hone the ear.
Play narrows into precision; resistance reveals its quiet mercy.
Form becomes a place one returns to, no longer to escape, but to listen.

PART III

Epiphanies in Life

Quiet Realizations Amid the Ordinary

Epiphanies in Life slows time enough to see what was already there.
These poems attend long enough for the ordinary to crack: soil, schedule, the word said twice.
Light doesn't interrupt—it reveals.
From craft's precision, eyes adjust—attention becomes the aperture, and gratitude finds its object.

III.1
Providence's Tomorrow

Day by day we're faced with pain,
Body's bane is not the drain.
Daily hurts while felt and real,
Silent mental lapse does steal
Spirit's power to plan and think,
Yet eclipse o'er heaven's brink
By joy, along with sorrow—
Providence's tomorrow.

Pain and joy share the same horizon; tomorrow remains untouched, already held.

Deliverance II.4

III.2
Time's Power

Excavating bit by bit,
On a slope afraid I'll slip,
All I have is my own wit,
So must rest and think a bit.

Much refreshed my mind now lit,
Coupled with enduring grit,
Double down then I must quit,
Else this hole becomes a pit.

Halfway done I now must knit,
Empty space with nature's kit,
Gently place as they befit,
Sprouts of Providence's writ.

Nurture, cherish, ponder, sit:
Time's the silent player's skit.
Other things are but a whit,
Farmer's wisdom ne'er omit.

Digging pauses, waiting does its own work, and growth occurs where effort loosens its grip.

Redemptions V.1

III.3

Divine Ooze

Poke me, prod me what comes forth?
Always, only, and henceforth,
Scripture oozes from my soul,
Bible teachings that cajole.

So you ask me, "Whence, why, how,
Should I now His truth avow?"
Yes embrace the fact He lives,
Knowledge resurrection gives.

But the hinge is, Whence the power?"
That gives rise to faith's small flower—
Focus changed by him who's won—
Sin, its struggle in him are done.

What emerges was planted long ago. Faith speaks before it is asked to explain itself.

III.4
Really Rhapsody Redacted

Say “really really” to me now,
then really, really I will bow,
and really, really genuflect,
it “really really” does affect
me, really, really everywhere,
yes, really, really savoir faire,
for “really really’s” all around,
I really, really like that sound,
so really, really you could say,
two “really really’s” make my day,
then really, really I will clap,
I really, really will not slap,
for really, really I delight,
in “really really’s” day or night.

So really, really come what may,
I’ll really, really hold at bay,
my really, really rigid ways,
won’t really, really say always,
“Just really really’s, nothing more,
I’m really, really such a bore,”
so really, really I will change,
it will be painful, stretch my range,
yet it will mold a new franchise,
no longer shall I make my prize,
to say by rote until I die,
meaningless words, to them goodbye.
Yet true deliverance shall come,
I really, really won’t succumb.

Repetition multiplies until it collapses under its own weight, leaving silence newly audible.

III.5

Really Rhapsody Redacted Rejoinder—When Copilot Got It Wrong

You really, really got it light,
So really, really it's not right;
Though "really really" is what's said,
Reads "really, really" in your head.

Clarification follows misfire. Even correction joins the game.

III.6

Educational Breeze—Finally Grateful

I never really worked that hard,
it always came so easy;
so early on was never jarred,
it was so easy-peasy.

This all was foreign to some "friends,"
they thought me a peculiar
aberration and misintends
of something not familiar.

But now reflection grabbed my life,
perceiving I most never,
was grateful for my mental rife,
gave Providence thanks ever.

Repentance—time to change my ways
and ponder on my blessing;
distance dazing from my days,
with thanks not window dressing.

Ease taken for granted becomes its own blindness. Reflection turns memory, and gratitude cracks open the gift given.

III.7
Prophecy's Perplexities

Throughout veiled history of mankind
Loom the prayers of prophets divined
In hidden terms, that belie belief,
Who tickle men's ears in vain relief.

Still, other prophets expound true truth,
But by fallen man adjudged uncouth.
Humanity's race from Adam's curse
Drive oracle's zeal and prophets's verse.

Yet looking toward these unseen things,
Divining words whose true meaning stings
Real believers's tender hearts and minds
To comprehend the Word's word that binds.

Truth resists easy hearing. Words aimed heavenward return sharpened.

III.8

Dead End's Illusion

Gentle slope ahead.
Wall hinders progress forward—
Illusion. Turn right.

The obstruction was never final. Direction arrives sideways.

Coda

Eight quiet breaks—Providence to illusion—pair moment with meaning.
The ordinary slows long enough to show its seams.
Recognition arrives sideways; what blocked the way was never final.

PART IV

Hope Amid Trials

Turns from Shadow to Steady Grace

Hope Amid Trials enters shadow—grief, despair, loss that returns.
These poems do not rush relief.
Darkness is met, not solved; grace appears as presence rather than escape.
From epiphany's stillness, the soul steps into shadow—and something refuses to let go.

IV.1

Year's Transition

Old year closing fast approaching,
New year coming faster still;
Tired, plodding somnambulation
Turned to dancing, life will fill.

Now the days that lie before me
Will be racing beneath my feet.
LORD please let me savor living
Before the end comes bittersweet.

Time accelerates without asking permission; the prayer is simply to notice.

IV.2
From Despair to Hope

Oh deep despair beyond all hope
Perchance my soul should feel
Immense entangled ponderous grief
That naught on earth can heal
Nay bitter portions do not seal
One's life to only sorrow
For grace immeasurably gives
The strength to face tomorrow

Despair tightens its hold, then—without announcement—something else stands nearby.

Deliverance V.3

IV.3
Furnace Warmth

Today I had a simple, child's delight
My senses danced as I turned off the light:
Furnace warm air gently warmed my backside;
Exterior's cold—it's warm here inside.

Comfort drifts in unnoticed. Shelter proves itself without argument.

IV.4
Fear Erased

My obsession taking hold—
Poem's focus, verse's gold.
Fears abate of lacking rhyme,
Stumbling rhythm, missing chime.

Deep night's day is lacking fear
For mind's sway abandons drear;
Dread is gone, delight has come
Hope has swapped with spirit's glum.

Attention narrows, fear recedes, and the mind forgets what it had been rehearsing.

IV.5

October's Rain

The rain does fall in cold relief
Unneeded by the ground,
As it calls out and softly cries
For all its roots are drown.

Saturation overwhelms what once needed water. Nature mirrors grief's excess.

IV.6

My Mother's Gift

You poured your life full into mine
And mothered me along,
The insecure, dependent boy
From years ago is gone.
So though God moved you off this earth
To your eternal home,
The boy you grew, the man you made—
Able to stand alone.

What was given remains active. Absence does not undo formation.

IV.7

Grieving Cord's Gold

The heavy cords of grief now take their hold,
A bitter brew consumed both dark and deep.
Yet every verse begins its turn to gold.
The story that my mother often told,
Is ours to treasure and is ours to keep;
The heavy cords of grief now take their hold.
The rain outside is biting, sharp and cold,
The roots that drown begin to cry and weep,
Yet every verse begins its turn to gold.
No longer by a stupid lie controlled,
While tired somnambulants do soundly sleep,
The heavy cords of grief now take their hold.
The rhythm rhyming joker grows quite bold,
Though up the mountain path is very steep,
Yet every verse begins its turn to gold.
The Savior's hand has bought the chosen fold,
What mercy sows, the faithful soul shall reap;
The heavy cords of grief now take their hold,
Yet every verse begins its turn to gold.

Grief tightens again and again, yet each return reveals a glint—its heavy cords quietly yielding mercy's gold.

IV.8
Inescapable Grief

Oh, inescapable grief!
Oh, insurmountable sorrow!
Where is my deliverer?
A bitter portion binds me;
Strong cords hold me fast.
I am incapable of escape;
There is none to rescue.
I am hopeless O LORD:
Be thou my hope.

No exit appears. The plea itself becomes the path.

Deliverance V.4

Coda

Eight descents—year to grief—each met without release.
Grace holds where answers thin; the loom keeps working its pattern.
The reader leaves wounded, upright, and still in motion.

PART V

Faithful Reflections

Affirmations of Providence in the Everyday

Faithful Reflections takes the long view—sovereignty, prayer, mercy woven through days.
These poems speak after trial, not above it.
What endures is named quietly: trust practiced, Providence walked with.
From repetition and return, the spirit remembers how it has been carried.

V.1
God’s Sovereignty

The bow’s been strung,
Arrow’s been shot,
Outcome not due
To die or lot.
Sovereign Lord
Made bow and man,
Superintends
Your lifelong plan.
Psalms 127:3-5; *3 John* 4

Flight begins long before release. Guidance precedes motion.

V.2

A Child's Answered Prayer

When I was 5-6, my parents bought me a GI Joe with a parachute. I spent the afternoon carefully wrapping up the parachutist and throwing him, as high as I could. Then I watched GI Joe float down from the sky.

After many throws, the GI Joe got wrapped around a telephone line that came into our house. The GI Joe was way too high for me, and I had no way to get him down. We had been talking about prayer in Sunday School, that no prayer was too small for God. So I laid down directly beneath my entangled GI Joe and I prayed to my Heavenly Father, "Dear God, please get my GI Joe down for me." I waited. What seemed like forever was probably 10 minutes, if that long.

Believing that God was not going to answer my prayer, I called out to my father, "Dad, my GI Joe is wrapped around the wire!" My dad, at that time in my life the biggest and strongest man in the world, came out and held and braced a ladder so that I could climb up to get him. At the top I carefully and slowly reached out to untangle the parachute.

In a moment of time, before I touched the parachute, everything changed. A gust of wind freed GI Joe! Those few words do not do justice to the event: In a blaze of rapid swings around the wire, first one way and then another, in multiple rotations, in a choreographed ballet of definitive and guided movement, GI Joe was freed. Freed more beautifully and effortlessly than I could have ever done. I have never doubted the existence of God since then, for in that serene moment, I watched GI Joe float down from the sky

Help arrives choreographed, long remembered as wind rather than force.

V.3
Mercy's Love

The love of Jesus this I know,
Not just the Bible tells me so:
Deliverance by death's love came,
His life's love now—never the same.

For He by mercy's love did save
With love's new life to me He gave.
Now gospel's struggle does begin:
Mercy's love in Adam's din.

Love does not end struggle; it changes what struggle means.

Deliverance IV.3

V.4
Tranquility

Alone - solitude;
A state of mind more than place.
Tranquil thoughts possess.

Quiet settles without geography. Solitude teaches location of the soul.

V.5
Thanksgiving Gratitude

Now to Him
who has most graciously
given us all things
pertaining both to this life
and the life to come,
we give thanks.

Gratitude gathers what was already given. Thanks completes the gift.

V.6
Christmas Welcome

This Christmas Day we welcome You
With love from God made manifest
By newborn Babe born in our midst
Son incarnate at God's behest

God enters without force. Welcome becomes worship.

V.7
Attuned to Grace

A perfect day begins attuned
To Jesus and His book,
And then I turn to other things
To outward take a look.
My spouse, my friends, my job – these three –
Routinely fill my day.
But starting with the first thing first
Makes perfect each step's way.

The day finds its pitch early, and everything else listens.

V.8

Children of God's Plan

I love my children
One and all
Married or single
Whatever befall
If they have children
Their kids are grand
It's all a part
Of God's great plan

Love widens naturally. Trust names the pattern only after seeing it.

Coda

Eight affirmations name what testing has already taught.
Not loud, not rare—near.
The cycle does not close; it walks on.

Between Ending and Beginning—

New Year's Hope

Here comes the New Year
Just like the last one except—
Unknown days greet us

Envoi

The circle widens even further: from first grin to last plea.
Nothing settled, everything said, nothing left unsaid.
Whimsy, craft, epiphany, trial, Providence—the inward pattern
echoing with every step—and the poems keep walking with us.

APPENDIX A
The Five Cycles of Redemptions Refrain

Redemptions Refrain unfolds in five cycles, each tracing a distinct movement of redemption.

These cycles are not stages to be completed, nor depths to be plumbed, but refrains that repeat. They do not descend; they recur—meeting the reader again as life continues, deepening not by crisis, but by return.

Where *Redemptions* explored breadth, and *Deliverance* explored depth,
Redemptions Refrain explores reach: how far grace extends into daily life.

I - Whimsy and Satire—Laughter That Steadies

Here redemption's refrain often begins lighter than expected. Here, humor loosens what has tightened—beards, pies, media absurdities, verse addiction. These poems do not trivialize life's weight; they prepare the soul to carry it. Laughter becomes grounding, not escape. Grace first appears as relief. The grin steadies before the work begins.

II – Poetic Craft and Challenge—Form That Resists, Then Frees

Words push back. Meter constrains. Rhyme demands attention. This cycle enters the workshop, where discipline reveals its quiet mercy. What once felt like restriction becomes structure; what resisted becomes release. Here redemption's refrain is practiced daily—not by inspiration alone, but by submission to form. Freedom arrives not by breaking rules, but by learning how faithfully to keep them.

III – Epiphanies in Life—The Ordinary Cracks Open

Nothing dramatic happens here. And yet—everything changes. These poems attend to time, soil, repetition, routine. They listen long enough for light to break through the ordinary. Redemption's refrain in this cycle is recognition: seeing what was always there. Grace does not interrupt life. It reveals it.

IV – Hope Amid Trials—Grace That Refuses to Let Go

Here the poems revisit—grief, despair, unanswered questions, and loss that returns. Hope is not declared. It is clung to again. This cycle does not promise relief, only presence. Grace appears not as rescue, but as endurance. Redemption's refrain here is stubborn: the refusal of grace to release its hold.

V – Faithful Reflections—Providence Walks with Us Daily

The final cycle widens the lens. Not triumph, but trust. These poems affirm what trial has tested—that Providence is not rare, loud, or theatrical, but faithful, quiet, and near. Redemption's refrain here is continuity. Life goes on—held, guided, sustained. The pattern does not end. It walks with us.

APPENDIX B

Redemptions Refrain

A Reader's Guide

This Reader's Guide explains how the book is arranged, why it differs in emphasis from the earlier volumes, and offers simple ways to read the poems so the structural choices feel intentional rather than accident

Relationship to the earlier books

- *Redemptions* moved broadly across themes—its aim was breadth: to introduce the range of the "redemption's refrain" pattern.
- *Deliverance* dug inward—probing depth and the interior work of deliverance.
- *Redemptions Refrain* is about reach: how far grace goes into the everyday. The Parts are arranged not as a plunge or ascent, but as a walk—from lightness toward steady trust—so the reader experiences grace widening through lived days rather than through escalating intensity.

Because of that intent you will notice a couple of structural choices here that differ from the earlier volumes:

1. Order as movement, not taxonomy. Poems are grouped to produce a felt movement—from loosened grip (Part I) into

the discipline of craft (Part II), then into the patient noticing of the ordinary (Part III), through trial (Part IV) and into faithful reflection (Part V). That ordering sometimes required relocating pieces so each Part reads as a refrain with internal coherence rather than as a mere topical cluster.

2. Refrain over stage. Where earlier books sometimes read like sequences of stages to be completed, this volume emphasizes redemption's refrain: the pattern of return. A poem may appear to "fit" in more than one Part; its placement here is chosen to strengthen the particular refrain the Part foregrounds.
3. Readerly options added. Appendix B is written to make those choices visible so readers can follow an intended arc or take other paths freely.

How to read this book

- Linear—follow the arc. Read Part I → V to experience the widening movement from whimsy to Providence. This is the path that most closely embodies the book's statement about "reach."
- Cycle-focus—dwell in a refrain. Spend a day or week in one Part (for example, return repeatedly to Part II to practice attention and rhythm). The refrains are designed to deepen with repetition.
- Thematic hops—read by need. Open where you are: grief (Part IV), instruction (Part II), or thanksgiving (Part V). Because refrains repeat, a single poem can both comfort and instruct.

What changed and why

- Some poems are positioned differently here than in the prior volumes to emphasize reach rather than resolution. When a poem reappears, it is not repeating a breakthrough but rehearsing a truth—how grace returns while life continues. The reader is meant to recognize the poem not as déjà vu, but as familiarity: the same voice speaking again in a different day.

- Appendix A and this guide explain those moves so the reader understands the intention: placement is chosen for felt effect and pastoral usefulness rather than rigid classification.

A note on use

- If you're reading for craft: linger in Part II and the linked exercises (meter, villanelle, form).
- If you're reading for consolation: Part IV and Part V offer sequences that hold sorrow and practice trust without flattening either.
- If you're reading devotionally: use the bullet points in the Introduction as a prompt for daily reflection and move into whichever Part your day's life most resembles.

Redemptions Refrain is meant to be both map and companion: a sequence you may follow, and a set of refrains you may revisit. Readers moving through the volumes together need not proceed linearly; these poems are written to be entered where life currently stands, not only where the book progresses.

APPENDIX C

Blessing and Curse

The Pattern of Redemptions Refrain

	Cycle Name Focus	**Curse** Bondage/ Constraint *Quote*	**Blessing** Freedom/Grace *Quote*	**Key Outcome/ Redemption** *Quote*
I	**Whimsy and Satire** Playful nudges at life's quirks	**Life's Weight** Pressure, clenching, heaviness *His beard being large, 'Bout the size of a barge (I.1)*	**Laughter's Release** Humor loosens, grin grounded *First world stuff, don't matter—I'll get buff (I.2)*	**Seriousness becomes Steadiness** *'gotta make your mind delight in rhyme (I.7)*
II	**Poetic Craft and Challenge** The pull of words and their playful tensions	**Word's Resistance** Meter constrains, rhyme demands *Villanelle did accost my being whole (II.2)*	**Form's Freedom** Discipline sharpens, form releases *comes poet's gain, divinely infused (II.1)*	**Constraint becomes Companion** *Together we'll purr with the felines (II.6)*
III	**Epiphanies in Life** Quiet Realizations Amid the Ordinary	**Ordinary Routine** Day's repeat, flatness *Say "really really" to me now (III.4)*	**Recognition's Light** Ordinary cracks open *Time's the silent player's skit (III.2)*	**Mundane becomes Doorway** *Illusion. Turn right (III.8)*

	Cycle Name Focus	**Curse** Bondage/ Constraint *Quote*	**Blessing** Freedom/Grace *Quote*	**Key Outcome/ Redemption** *Quote*
IV	**Hope Amid Trials** Turns from Shadows to Steady Grace	**Shadow's Grip** Despair tightens, inescapable loss *Oh, inescapable grief! (IV.8)*	**Graces Refusal** Grace endures, stubborn presence *For grace immeasurably gives The strength to face tomorrow (IV.2)*	**Wound becomes Witness** *Exterior cold—it's warm here inside (IV.3)*
V	**Faithful Reflections** Affirmations of Providence in the Everyday	**Solitary Struggle** Alone, unanswered *Alone – solitude (V.4)*	**Providence's Companionship** Providence faithful, quiet near *A gust of wind freed GI Joe! (V.2)*	**Uncertainty becomes Trust** *A perfect day begins attuned To Jesus and His book (V.7)*

The overarching message is that true freedom is found when grace extends its reach into every dimension of daily life—from laughter through craft, revelation through trial, to Providence trusted day by day.

Note on Terms

Atonement – Christ's exchange of His righteousness for our sin, reconciling us to God.

Coda – a concluding passage that gathers the cycle's threads, offering rest without full closure.

Couplet – two successive rhyming lines, often used to close a thought with a sudden click of recognition.

Deliverance – redemption lived over time; freedom not only declared but received and endured by grace.

Despair Redacted – despair fully faced, yet crossed out by mercy; remembered, but denied final authority.

Doxology – a brief expression of praise to God, often marking the turn from struggle to gratitude.

Envoi – a short stanza sending off the work, often with a nod to its intent or recipient.

Exchange – The cross's great trade: His life for mine, my sin for his righteousness.

Form – in both poetry and faith, the accepted limits through which true freedom is discovered.

Grace – the unearned gift by which both life and art are set free.

Hinge poem – a spare piece that pivots the sequence, turning lament toward grace with a single breath.

Lament – an honest outpouring of sorrow, the soul's cry that grace quietly answers.

Loop Poem –the last word in each line becomes the first in the next; the last word loops to the first word.

Monorhyme – a poem or stanza in which every line ends on the same rhyme sound.

Ode – a lyric celebration of a subject, turning the mundane into something sung.

Providence – God's quiet governance when strength fails; the hand that leads where effort cannot.

Quatrain – a four-line stanza, the quiet workhorse of English hymnody and complaint.

Redemption – deliverance from any bondage through mercy and transformation.

Refrain – a return that bears meaning; in poetry and faith, what repeats until grace breaks or carries it.

Shaped poem – a poem whose visual arrangement on the page participates in its meaning.

Sin – the will's turning from divine order, healed only by grace.

Spare poem – a piece deliberately thinned to bone so that every remaining word rings like struck flint.

Triptych -- a three-part poetic sequence functioning as unified statement. The Humanity Triptych traces descent, transcendence, and communion through three villanelles.

Villanelle – a nineteen-line form built on two refrains and two repeating rhymes.

www.ingramcontent.com/pod-product-compliance
Lightning Source LLC
LaVergne TN
LVHW020658100826
845148LV00012B/2558

* 9 7 9 8 3 8 5 2 7 5 4 0 3 *